*Well-behaved women
seldom make history.*
—Laurel Thatcher Ulrich

Sonia Sotomayor

KATHLEEN KRULL

interior illustrations by
Angela Dominguez

BLOOMSBURY
NEW YORK   LONDON   NEW DELHI   SYDNEY

To Dr. Donna L. Keefe,
a woman who breaks the rules

First published in the United States of America in June 2015
by Bloomsbury Children's Books
www.bloomsbury.com

Bloomsbury is a registered trademark of Bloomsbury Publishing Plc

For information about permission to reproduce selections from this book, write to
Permissions, Bloomsbury Children's Books, 1385 Broadway, New York, New York 10018
Bloomsbury books may be purchased for business or promotional use. For information on bulk purchases please contact
Macmillan Corporate and Premium Sales Department at specialmarkets@macmillan.com

Library of Congress Cataloging-in-Publication Data
Krull, Kathleen, author.
Women who broke the rules : Sonia Sotomayor / by Kathleen Krull ; illustrated by Angela Dominguez.
pages   cm
ISBN 978-0-8027-3798-4 (paperback) • ISBN 978-0-8027-3797-7 (hardcover)
1. Sotomayor, Sonia, 1954—Juvenile literature. 2. Judges—United States—Biography—Juvenile literature.
3. Hispanic American judges—Biography—Juvenile literature. I. Dominguez, Angela N., illustrator. II. Title.
KF8745.S67K78 2015   347.73'2634—dc23   [B]   2014019267

Art created with gouache and ink on Bristol board and digitally
Typeset in Beaufort
Book design by Nicole Gastonguay

Printed in China by Leo Paper Products, Heshan, Guangdong
2 4 6 8 10 9 7 5 3 1 (paperback)
2 4 6 8 10 9 7 5 3 1 (hardcover)

All papers used by Bloomsbury Publishing, Inc., are natural, recyclable products
made from wood grown in well-managed forests. The manufacturing processes
conform to the environmental regulations of the country of origin.

TABLE OF CONTENTS

1 ★ HOT PEPPER

A girl grows up in a tough neighborhood. Her poor, immigrant parents don't speak English and don't get along. She tackles a serious illness . . . and rises, rises, rises to become one of the country's guiding lights.

How did Sonia Sotomayor *do* that?

"My sister," her younger brother said, "was tough as nails." He would know. She beat him up all the time. (But she was also his protector at school. Anyone who wanted to pick on him had to fight her first.)

"I've spent my whole life," Sonia once wrote, "learning how to do things that were hard for me."

Life was hard almost from the time she was born on June 25, 1954, in the Bronx, part of New York City. She grew up in redbrick public housing projects for people with little money. Sonia was so feisty as a toddler that her nickname was Aji, or Hot Pepper. Her parents worried that too much energy would get her in trouble.

Both parents had left all their family and friends behind in Puerto Rico. A group of islands in the Caribbean Sea, Puerto Rico is not a state—yet. It has belonged to the United States since 1898 and is the poorest territory under its rule. Many of its Spanish-speaking people have moved away in search of better lives.

Sonia's mother worked as a nurse; her father worked in a factory. The couple mostly fought. Angry about her husband's alcoholism, Sonia's mother worked longer and longer hours away from home.

Sonia's safety zone was her grandmother's apartment. It smelled like the garlic and onions that went into *sofrito*, the spicy Puerto Rican sauce. Her *abuelita*'s encouragement helped Sonia "imagine the most improbable of possibilities for my life."

Sonia faced her hardest challenge at age seven.

One day she fainted in church. She was hospitalized and underwent horribly painful tests. The diagnosis, alas, was diabetes. The doctor explained that her body wasn't producing enough of a chemical called insulin. Every day, to stay alive, she would have to have insulin injections.

But Sonia's father's hands trembled, and her mother was seldom home. So she learned how to give herself the shots. She practiced injecting an orange at first. Soon she was a pro, relieved that she didn't have to bother her parents. "The last thing I wanted was for them to fight about me," she said later.

Diabetes sometimes cuts lives short. Sonia had a feeling that she had no time to waste. Even at an early age, she wanted goals.

Her father died when she was nine. Her mother worked longer hours than ever to support herself and her two young children.

The children's education became her mother's obsession. She made a point of speaking only English with them at home. And at great sacrifice, she bought them every single volume of the *Encyclopaedia Britannica*. With its detailed pictures and information, it expanded Sonia's horizons.

She started hanging out at the library. Her favorite books were the Nancy Drew mysteries, with the girl detective who risks danger to solve crimes. Nancy broke rules that usually kept girls on the sidelines. She was active, outspoken, brainy, and not afraid to show it.

Sonia was set on being a detective like Nancy, a real one on a police force. She seemed to meet the requirements: "I was a keen observer and listener. I picked up on clues. I figured things out logically, and I enjoyed puzzles."

Her doctor squashed that plan. At that time, police detective was on the list of jobs too active for someone with diabetes.

Sonia didn't give up. She also adored *Perry Mason*, a TV courtroom drama. Our legal system is so complex that people need lawyers—experts in the law—to help. Perry was a wise lawyer who seldom lost a case. Sonia saw attorneys as heroes—arguing, solving problems with brainpower, using the law to right wrongs. Plus, Perry usually worked safely inside, in a courtroom.

Perfect! "I was going to college," she said, "and I was going to become an attorney, and I knew that when I was ten."

One day a *Perry Mason* episode ended with a shot of the judge in charge of the trial. "I realized that the judge was the most important player in the room," she said. He—it was always a man—was the boss of everyone, even the lawyers.

How does a person even *become* a judge? Sonia had no idea, but it was probably going to involve breaking some rules.

2 MAKING CHOICES

One year Sonia's apartment became infested with giant cockroaches. It gave her a lifelong fear of creepy crawly things.

But the public housing projects were mostly safe then, even though danger lurked. Sonia grew up watching how people handled their problems: "And you saw kids making choices."

One of them was her best friend, her cousin Nelson. He was smarter than she was, but he made bad choices. He became addicted to drugs and died before he was thirty. This was not going to happen to Sonia.

At school she rarely got in trouble. She had too much respect for the Catholic nuns and their strict rules. (Actually, it was more like fear.)

Her fifth-grade teacher sparked her. She put up gold stars whenever a student excelled. Sonia set out to get the most stars, even though she wasn't the best student. But in an unusual move, she asked a girl named Donna, the smartest kid in her class, for tips on how to study. It worked. Sonia earned more stars, and she learned that getting help was cool.

Like other kids, she loved the Beatles (her favorite was Ringo). She laughed at *The Three Stooges* on TV. She was a die-hard fan of the New York Yankees.

But she also thought ahead. Realizing that being a lawyer meant speaking in front of others, she started reading the Bible to others at her church, something girls were newly allowed to do. At thirteen, her hero was Robert F. Kennedy, an idealistic lawyer running for president in 1968.

She was so unlike other girls that her eighth-grade teacher was baffled: "The girl's ambitions, odd as they seem," the nun wrote in Sonia's yearbook, "are to become an attorney and someday marry. Hopefully, she wishes to be successful in both fields."

Once in high school, Sonia didn't do well at first. But she worked extra-hard, again asked for help, and was soon on her way.

Her social life included a boy-friend named Kevin. He brought her a white rose every day at school, until he finally confessed he'd been clipping them from her uncle's rosebushes.

She wasn't active in the school's small Latino club. She and her Latino friends weren't embarrassed by their heritage, but they didn't go out of their way to celebrate it either. Images of Puerto Ricans at the time were often negative. In *West Side Story*, a popular Broadway musical and movie, they were shown as gang members and criminals, not that smart, speaking broken English.

But Sonia did join the debate team. It was fun to make an argument and to "read" people by watching their body language. She even figured out how to argue with teachers—without getting in trouble—when she felt that they were being unfair.

Her kitchen table was a meeting place for Sonia's friends to yak about events in the news. Her mother would get home after her long workday and feed the group pork chops, rice, and beans.

To no one's surprise, Sonia graduated at the top of her class. What now?

One of her best friends, a Chinese American boy a year older, told her to follow him to an Ivy League college. These private schools—Harvard, Princeton, and six others—were considered the best. They had ivy-covered buildings and were hard to get into . . . and cost more than she could ever afford. They were mostly white and male, but they were growing more diverse—and providing scholarship money.

Sonia's friend warned that such a fancy college would be hard for her. But he urged her on. She didn't need that much urging. She had seen the movie *Love Story* and had fallen in love with Harvard in Massachusetts.

Reality was different. After taking the train to Harvard, she was so nervous that she fled during her appointment—even though the school had already admitted her.

Harvard took that as a no.

Luckily, Sonia also loved the leafy campus of Princeton University in the town of Princeton, New Jersey. She was so jazzed to be offered a full scholarship that she splurged on a new coat—a white raincoat with fake fur trim.

But college nearly knocked her flat.

Part of the problem was that she'd rarely been out of a big city. At first she couldn't tell a cow from a horse. What were those creepy chirps outside her dorm's window? (Someone eventually told her about crickets.)

Partly, it was how much harder her classes were. Shocked

to receive a C on her first paper, she realized her basic skills needed work.

It was all so strange. "I felt like an alien landing in a different universe," she said. In 1972, there were only a few Latino students and no Latino professors or staff. Women were greatly outnumbered too.

For all these reasons, Sonia spent her first year too embarrassed to ask questions. Fear of failing drove her to work feverishly.

Her hangout became Princeton's magnificent library. She mastered ten new words a day. She memorized grade-school

grammar books to make sure her writing followed the rules of English, not Spanish.

She'd never been to a bookstore before. But she found her local Barnes & Noble and bought *Alice's Adventures in Wonderland* (she'd never heard of it until that year) and other classics.

She also accepted help from a professor who offered to teach her how to think, not just memorize.

She majored in history but took all kinds of classes. Now she earned almost all As. Her worst ordeal was the psychology lab. It required her to hold rats. With her fear of creepy

crawly things, she screamed and ran out of the room. (But she still managed to get a good grade.)

She blossomed, going from being shy to speaking out. Ironically, it was on this mostly all-white campus that she found her Puerto Rican "roots." She cochaired an organization working for more opportunity for Puerto Rican students.

Princeton's president began turning to Sonia for advice on Latino issues. He went on to hire its first Latino administrator and professor.

She still wanted to be a lawyer, maybe even a judge. One day she read about something she'd never heard of: the Supreme Court. These were the most important judges in the land, nine scholars in long black robes—all men, of course. They ruled on the hardest cases.

And she found out how you become a judge in any court. It's not a job you can apply for; when you're very old, you can get appointed or nominated. Tricky.

She got her first taste of judging as part of a panel that gave penalties for stolen library books, cheating, rowdiness, and the like.

For her combination of strong grades and outside activities she was awarded the highest prize a student can win at graduation. Her work had paid off, and she was closer to her goals.

But you can't be a lawyer without going to law school, and law school was *hard*.

First, Sonia married her boyfriend, Kevin, on his way to becoming a biologist. Then, in 1976, she entered law school. Yale University gave her a full scholarship. She studied nonstop, breaking rarely to play with their dog, Star.

Her classmates were mostly wealthy. She seemed older and more mature than they were, perhaps because of her difficult childhood or because she was married.

But in her first year she was still often frightened and didn't raise her hand. The lack of bathrooms didn't help.

Having the women's bathrooms be such a long walk away was a constant reminder that Yale was one of the first law schools to admit women.

Once she found her footing, Sonia was as outspoken as ever. One professor called her "extremely warm and very tough . . . an unusually brainy student even in this brainy group."

Not everyone approved. Some accused her of arguing "like a man." She didn't hesitate or apologize the way women were expected to.

Like the other law students, she tried to line up a job while still in school. Her quest didn't go well. At one firm, she felt insulted. The interviewer said that she had gotten into Yale only because she was Puerto Rican—ignoring her stellar record at Princeton.

Sonia was angry enough to fight back. She filed a complaint, and the law firm was ordered to apologize.

Then came the night of the free cheddar cheese cubes. Curious, not to mention hungry, she was lured into a meeting room. The New York District Attorney was recruiting Yale students for public service jobs. She stayed to talk, and he called her the next day. Would Sonia like to be an assistant district attorney, someone who works for the government in criminal cases?

Others warned her that she'd make no money in public service compared to private practice. But money was never her dream. This offer was too spine tingling to pass up. Out of this random meeting over cheese and crackers came her first job.

Sonia pounced at the chance to be back in New York City in 1979, fighting a wave of crimes. She was one of the "ducklings," the newbies. She had a hundred cases on her desk at a time, working from seven in the morning until ten at night.

She started off handling petty offenses—disorderly conduct, minor assault, graffiti. It was her job to prove that the people on trial really had shoplifted or trespassed.

Just weeks after she started, she was the first in her group of ducklings to have a case go to trial. She lost that case but

won her second. Then she moved up to working on more serious crimes, like murder.

One day Sonia discovered a kind of superpower. She realized that she could use emotion, not just facts, in her arguments. She saw how helpful it was in persuading people. It meant she had to pay attention with a laser-like focus.

She never lost a case again.

Her first murder trial was about a man known as the Tarzan Murderer. He swung into apartments through windows

and then robbed and murdered people. She won, and he was sentenced to sixty-seven years in prison.

In her four years on this job, she broke rules women were supposed to follow. Some male lawyers assumed she was a secretary, in the courtroom to type up notes. She learned to never let on that she knew how to type.

Some may have wanted to use her old nickname, Hot Pepper. They called her tough and ruthless. They were simply not used to seeing a woman argue in court, especially one with her intense focus. She reacted by trying to keep her sense of humor and balance.

Working such long hours left her with little time for salsa dancing, baseball games, or her marriage. She and Kevin ended up divorcing.

By 1983 it was time for a change.

In search of new ways to catch bad guys, Sonia joined a private law firm. It helped companies go after those making cheap copies of their goods.

This job was dangerous enough to occasionally require a bulletproof vest. If the firm knew a shipment of fakes was coming in, Sonia sometimes went directly to the warehouse to have the goods seized.

In her hairiest case—a shipment arriving in Chinatown—the criminals ran off. That day, Sonia showed up with police

and actually had to hop on one of their motorcycles and give chase.

Her firm made her a partner—a rare promotion for women then. She also did more than her share to help poor clients for free. She was a frequent speaker, urging women and Latinos to go into law. In her personal life, she was the fondest possible aunt and godmother, taking the kids in her life to shows and museums to expand their horizons.

As nine years passed, there were giddy whispers about Sonia, whispers that made her wince: she was on the fast track to becoming a judge. For fear of being called crazy, she never spoke of that dream. She knew about the luck and hurdles involved. If this ever did happen to her, it would be a lot later in life.

Actually, no.

The senator from New York State had Sonia on his radar. In 1991 he recommended her to the president. The following year she was confirmed as a New York federal district judge. At the stunning age of thirty-eight she had made her dream come true.

Sonia was the only Latino and the youngest judge in the state. Even she was startled. "It's very strange to wear the title 'judge,'" she said.

On her first day in court, about to speak from the bench, her knees knocked together. Could the microphone pick up the sound?

But the minute she jumped in with a question, she realized she'd be just fine.

For the next six years she judged cases on crimes involving illegal drugs and immigration offenses. Being a judge ruled!

Sonia's liveliest case came in 1995. Owners of the baseball teams wanted to cut the players' salaries, and the players went on strike—they stopped working. Even the World Series was canceled, and fans were outraged. It was Sonia to the rescue, ruling in favor of the players. Games resumed, and she became known as "the judge who saved baseball."

She was definitely soaring. In 1997 another president nominated her to the Court of Appeals. An appeal means asking a higher court to reverse a lower court's decision. It's sort of like appealing to one parent to change a rule made by your other parent.

This was such a promotion that she had to be approved by the United States Senate. It took more than a year. Opponents kept delaying, but eventually she was confirmed by a vote of sixty-seven to twenty-nine.

Over the next eleven years, she asked a lot of tough questions while judging thousands of cases. Sometimes she cut off lawyers who couldn't answer those questions. The lawyers used words like "bully," "nasty," and "a terror."

But as someone who worked for her pointed out: Sonia "doesn't tolerate unpreparedness, nor should she."

Her most famous case, in 2008, concerned firefighters. A group of white firefighters protested that their city had unfairly promoted minority firefighters. Sonia's ruling upheld, or agreed with, the city's action. (Though in the end, the Supreme Court overturned her ruling.)

One lovely April day the following year, Sonia was on her way to the gym. Her cell phone rang.

I t seemed that the White House was trying to reach her. When she got inside her car, she called the number she'd been given.

"My heart skipped a beat," she said. At age fifty-four, she was one of President Barack Obama's four candidates for the next Supreme Court judge.

That's right—one of nine of the most important judges in the country. By this time—*finally*—there were two women justices. Sonia's rivals for the job were all women, so one way or another, a third woman was about to join the court.

But being on the Supreme Court would be stressful. She'd be famous and lose her privacy, and her workload would be more ginormous than ever. Part of her wanted to withdraw from consideration.

What? A close friend pointed out how Sonia had always lacked role models. Now she could change that for those following her.

She stayed in the running.

A team from the White House checked her out from head to toe. They contacted her doctor and medical experts to see if diabetes would affect her work. No. Insulin injections and careful monitoring had kept it under control for decades.

Did she own anything that could cloud her judgment? No. She was never as wealthy as the people she had gone to school with, and she had no major investments—just a Greenwich Village condo.

Was she really that hard to get along with? No. The team interviewed many of her coworkers and was assured that this label was false.

Okay so far. But did Sonia ever break the law? Well, she did have that parking ticket. And like everyone in New York City, she freely admitted to jaywalking. But these weren't enough to count against her.

On May 26, 2009, the president himself called her in New York: she was his pick. She kept one hand on her chest, trying to stay calm.

She left for Washington immediately. She worked on her acceptance speech in the car, delivering it after only three hours of sleep. Her mother was with her, wiping away tears as the president announced the historic nomination.

In July she faced four solid days of piercing questions

from a Senate committee. They had to make sure she was Supreme Court—worthy.

Probably her biggest hurdle was a comment she'd made about being a "wise Latina." Senators wanted to know what this meant: "I would hope that a wise Latina woman with the richness of her experiences would more often than not reach a better conclusion than a white male who hasn't lived that life." Was she a racist? Was she saying that she would favor women and minorities in her rulings? This isn't what justices are supposed to do—they're supposed to use the Constitution as their guide.

Sonia assured the committee that she had the utmost respect for the Constitution. What she had meant was that she knew firsthand about prejudice and how it feels to be judged. She had lived through things other judges had not. She had a broader perspective on real life.

The Senate gave its stamp of approval by a vote of sixty-eight to thirty-one. Sonia Sotomayor became only the third woman and first Latino to sit on the highest court in the land.

What did it feel like to make history? While taking the oath of office, she said, "I felt as if an electric current were coursing through me."

Her first case hit her desk while she was still hiring four clerks and practicing baseball throwing twenty minutes a day. To her delight she'd been invited to throw the first pitch at Yankee Stadium a few weeks later. (On game day she performed perfectly, beaming at the crowds cheering for her.)

Typically, she was scared to death her first day on the bench, in awe of her eight companions. But she soon hit her stride. The justices often totally disagree, but she reported that "in person, we treat each other with respect and love."

People with a legal issue like to threaten, "I'm going to take this case all the way to the Supreme Court!" But the Supreme Court is extremely picky. It accepts only 1 percent of cases—the huge ones—that come before it. The issues involve civil rights, censorship, freedom of religion, the death penalty, the rights of criminal suspects, and much more.

Among her cases so far is one that reversed a lower court's ruling about immigration. On another case, the court decided that corporations can spend money to support or oppose political candidates. She also ruled on a case that upheld the Affordable Care Act, which provides Americans with health insurance.

Her hope was "to write opinions that will last the ages." Plus being a role model. "I would like there to be no child in America who grows up not knowing what the Supreme Court is," she said.

A bunch of Muppets from *Sesame Street* hang out in Sonia's chambers. "Pretending to be a princess is fun, but it is definitely not a career," she once told the show's viewers. Instead she suggested, "You can go to school and train to be a teacher, a lawyer, a doctor, an engineer, and even a scientist."

Or a judge.

★ SOURCES AND FURTHER READING ★

Books

(* especially for young readers)

Felix, Antonia. *Sonia Sotomayor: The True American Dream*. New York: Berkley Books, 2010.

* Gagne, Tammy. *What It's Like to Be Sonia Sotomayor/ Qué se siente al ser Sonia Sotomayor?* Hockessin, DE: Mitchell Lane Publishers, 2010.

* Gitlin, Martin. *Sonia Sotomayor: Supreme Court Justice*. Edina, MN: ABDO Publishing Company, 2011.

Greenhouse, Linda. *The U.S. Supreme Court: A Very Short Introduction*. New York: Oxford University Press, 2012.

Hartman, Gary, Roy Mersky, and Cindy L. Tate. *Landmark Supreme Court Cases: The Most Influential Decisions of the Supreme Court of the United States*. New York: Checkmark Books, 2006.

* Infobase Publishing. *Careers in Focus: Law*. New York: Ferguson Publishing, 2009.

* Krull, Kathleen. *A Kids' Guide to America's Bill of Rights: Curfews, Censorship, and the 100-Pound Giant*. New York: Avon, 1999.

* Madani, Hamed. *The Supreme Court and the Judicial Branch: How the Federal Courts Interpret Our Laws*. Berkeley Heights, NJ: Enslow Publishers, 2012.

* Shichtman, Sandra H. *Supreme Court Justices: Sonia Sotomayor*. Greensboro, NC: Morgan Reynolds Publishing, 2011.

Sotomayor, Sonia. *My Beloved World*. New York: Knopf, 2013.

* Williams, Zella. *Sonia Sotomayor: Supreme Court Justice/Sonia Sotomayor: Jueza de la Corte Suprema*. New York: The Rosen Publishing Group, 2011.

* Winter, Jonah. *Sonia Sotomayor: A Judge Grows in the Bronx/La Juez que Creció en el Bronx*. New York: Atheneum, 2009.

Websites

American Bar Association: **www.americanbar.org**
Princeton University: **www.princeton.edu**
Supreme Court of the United States: **www.supremecourt.gov**
United States Courts: **www.uscourts.gov**
"Who Is Sonia Sotomayor?" CNN: **www.cnn.com/2009/POLITICS/05/26/sotomayor.bio**
Yale Law School: **www.law.yale.edu**

★ INDEX ★